MW01121803

DETECTION DOGS
ON THE JOB

BY ROXANNE TROUP

The Child's World®
childsworld.com

Published by The Child's World®
1980 Lookout Drive • Mankato, MN 56003-1705
800-599-READ • www.childsworld.com

Photographs ©: Rich Legg/iStockphoto, cover, 1; Monika Wisniewska/
Shutterstock Images, 5; Andrew Link/Winona Daily News/AP Images, 6;
M. E. Giordano Photography/iStockphoto, 8; Kayla Overton/U.S. Army
Garrison-Hawaii Public Affairs, 9, 20; Marnie A. Pepper/USDA, 10; State
Farm CC2.0, 12; U.S. Customs and Border Protection, 14; Daniel Maurer/AP
Images, 15; Jessica Hill/AP Images, 16; Courtesy of the Oahu Army Natural
Resources Program, 18

ISBN 9781503816114

LCCN 2016946764

Printed in the United States of America
PA02318

TABLE OF CONTENTS

FAST FACTS

The Job

- Detection dogs use their sense of smell to find things. They are used for many different jobs.

- **Customs** detection dogs work in airports, train stations, and along borders. These dogs sniff out illegal goods.

- **Conservation** detection dogs help scientists find rare plants and animals.

- Medical detection dogs live with families who have children with medical conditions. The dogs help kids with **diabetes** and **allergies** stay safe.

- Some detection dogs work with police. They help find hidden stashes of illegal materials.

Training Time

- Customs dogs train for 10 to 13 weeks before they test to become official detection dogs.

- Conservation dogs go through training for four months. On the job, they often learn to follow new scents. Each new scent takes four more weeks of training.

- Medical detection dogs may train for up to two years.

Common Breeds

- Beagles
- Labrador retrievers
- Labradoodles and other allergy-friendly breeds

Famous Dogs

- Stella, a Staffordshire bull terrier from the United Kingdom, worked with police. She helped them find thousands of dollars of illegal money.
- Ruger, a detection dog in Zambia, was nearly blind. But she used her nose to help authorities stop elephant and rhino **poachers**.

Chapter 1

WICKET'S STORY

Wicket, a black Labrador retriever mix, jumped down from the truck. It was a warm and sunny spring morning in New York's Adirondack Mountains. Wicket stood with her **handler** at the edge of a forest. Wicket's handler clipped an orange vest onto Wicket's back. The vest helped the handler see Wicket while she worked. Wicket waited as her handler tucked a ball into her belt pack. Wicket did not jump for it. She was ready to work.

At her handler's word, Wicket trotted into the forest. Wicket was from Montana. She had never been in this forest before. A new smell floated past her nose. She turned her head but kept moving. Another smell floated past. With her nose in the air, Wicket sniffed quickly.

◀ Wicket, wearing her orange vest, sits at attention during a demonstration in 2012.

She was looking for the one smell she had spent weeks learning to recognize.

Conservation scientists had worked for years to protect the forests in the Adirondacks. Moose lived in the forests. The scientists thought the moose population in the mountains was growing. Now Wicket and her team were looking for proof of the growth.

▲ Moose were reintroduced to the Adirondack Mountains in the early 1900s.

▲ Wicket picks up a scent during a
mission in 2010.

But Wicket was not looking for moose. She was
searching for their **scat**. Scat can tell scientists a lot
about animals. It tells them what animals eat, where they
live, and even how healthy they are.

But the scent samples Wicket had trained with were
from the fall. Moose eat different plants in the spring.
Their scat smells different. Would Wicket be able to
help find the moose?

Chapter 2

THE NOSE KNOWS

S ome detection dogs start training at a young age. Other dogs, such as Wicket, are a little older when they begin. Dogs must have certain **traits** to be good detection dogs. They usually have lots of energy and excellent focus. Wicket had all the right traits when a handler found her at a shelter. The handler held a ball in front of Wicket's kennel. Wicket's eyes stayed focused on the ball the whole time. The trainer knew Wicket would be a great conservation dog.

Once dogs are picked to become conservation dogs, they begin scent training. Rogue was a Belgian sheepdog. As a conservation dog, she trained to find an important plant called Kincaid's lupine.

◀ **Conservation dogs and their trainers spend a lot of time outdoors.**

A rare type of butterfly lays its eggs on the plant. Rogue's handler put lupine leaves under Rogue's nose. Then the handler hid the leaves in a row of concrete blocks. Rogue put her nose over each block. When she smelled Kincaid's lupine, she sat. Each time Rogue was correct, her handler gave her a toy to play with.

Next, Rogue's handler put other scents in the unused blocks. Rogue needed to find the correct scent and ignore the others. She did! A few days later, Rogue's handler tried the test in an open field. Over the course of 25 days, Rogue only missed one Kincaid's lupine her handler hid. Rogue was ready to go to work.

Dogs are not the only ones that need training. They need human handlers who can direct and communicate with them. Skipper, a beagle, flew through his training as a customs dog. He learned how to smell different plants and foods that were illegal to bring into a country. But it took one year to find a handler who could control Skipper's energetic personality.

◀ A detection dog searches for a scent among concrete blocks.

▲ A beagle and her handler check a bag at an airport in San Francisco, California.

After a few months of training together, the team went to work searching bags and suitcases at an airport. In 2013, Skipper jumped onto a conveyor belt at the San Francisco, California, airport. He danced around a bag. Skipper's handler asked the owner of the bag to open it. Inside was a live giant snail. The snail is illegal in the United States. Each time Skipper found something illegal, his trainer gave him a treat.

Some customs dogs work with police. Atos is a German shepherd that works as a currency dog. He is trained to smell the ink and paper used to print money. He sniffs crates and cars before they are loaded onto ships.

▲ A currency dog sniffs out a stash of money in a car crossing the border from Switzerland to Germany.

Some detection dogs do not search for illegal things. Instead, they train as medical detection dogs. These dogs live with people with medical conditions. A yellow Labrador retriever named Riley goes everywhere with his young handler. When his handler goes to school, Riley goes, too. When the boy goes to the park, Riley is there. Riley's handler is allergic to peanuts. Being near them can send the boy to the hospital. Riley keeps his handler safe by sniffing out peanuts and alerting him when they are nearby.

Another yellow Labrador retriever helps a young boy who has diabetes. Alan's job is to alert the boy when his blood sugar changes. Alan sits in the stands with the boy's mom during his basketball practices. If the boy's blood sugar gets too low, Alan tugs on his leash. He nibbles on the boy's mom's hand. Thanks to Alan, the boy can keep his blood sugar at a safe level.

◄ A boy with a peanut allergy walks with his allergy detection dog.

Chapter 3

SUCCESS!

With her head high, Wicket led her handler through the mountain forest. Wicket is an air-scent dog. She does not work with her nose to the ground. She catches scents in the air and follows them. The scents become stronger as she gets closer to them.

Wicket changed direction. She then stopped and turned around. After walking a few feet, she stopped again and turned. She kept zigzagging beneath the trees looking for the place with the strongest scent. She sped up. Her tail wagged. Suddenly she stopped, sat, and looked at her handler.

Wicket's handler knelt down and saw that Wicket had found bear scat. Wicket had trained to find bear scat.

◄ **A conservationist takes notes on her detection dog's findings.**

But on this mission the team was looking for moose scat. Wicket's handler bagged the scat. She gave Wicket a ball as a reward. The two took some time to play. Soon they were off again with Wicket in the lead.

Wicket and her team worked hard. They covered a huge area over several weeks. The team searched for three days, took a day off, and then worked for three more. Eventually, their hard work paid off. Wicket and her team found 141 pieces of moose scat.

THINK ABOUT IT

- A lot of detection dogs are rescued from shelters. Why do you think that is?
- What are some of the traits dogs need to have in order to be good detection dogs?
- Detection dogs work in many different places. Where might you find a detection dog at work in your area?

◀ Wicket plays with her ball after a successful mission in 2010.

GLOSSARY

allergies (AL-ur-jeez): Allergies are reactions to things such as bee stings or peanuts. Detection dogs can help people with allergies avoid things that make them sick.

conservation (kahn-sur-VAY-shuhn): Conservation is the protection of wildlife and natural resources. Some conservation dogs search for endangered animals.

customs (KUHS-tuhmz): Customs is a place where officials check people and items entering a country. Customs dogs help keep illegal things out of a country.

diabetes (dye-uh-BEE-teez): Diabetes is a disease in which the body cannot control blood sugar correctly. People with diabetes take medicine to control their blood sugar.

handler (HAND-lur): A handler is a person who trains an animal. A detection dog and a handler form a team.

poachers (POHCH-urs): Poachers are people who hunt illegally. Detection dogs can be used to find poachers.

scat (SKAT): Scat is animal poop. Scientists use scat to learn about animals.

traits (TRAYTS): Traits are qualities that make people or animals different from one another. Certain traits make for better detection dogs.

TO LEARN MORE

Books

Castaldo, Nancy F. *Sniffer Dogs*. New York: Houghton Mifflin Harcourt, 2014.

Wadsworth, Ginger. *Poop Detectives*. Watertown, MA: Charlesbridge, 2016.

Wood, Alix. *Animal Handler*. New York: PowerKids, 2014.

Web Sites

Visit our Web site for links about detection dogs: childsworld.com/links

Note to Parents, Teachers, and Librarians: We routinely verify our Web links to make sure they are safe and active sites. So encourage your readers to check them out!

SELECTED BIBLIOGRAPHY

Bayne, Rachel. "Dog Detectives Are on the Case to Save Lives." *Oxford Mail News*. Newsquest, 25 Jan. 2014. Web. 30 Jun. 2016.

Eskenazi, Joe. "Dog Enforcement Agency: The Government's Illegal Food Detectors Sniff among Us." *SF Weekly*. SF Weekly, 9 Oct. 2013. Web. 30 Jun. 2016.

"Wicket." *Rescues2theRescue.org*. Working Dogs for Conservation, n.d. Web. 7 Jul. 2016.

INDEX

ABOUT THE AUTHOR

With a background in elementary education, Roxanne Troup writes engaging nonfiction for children of all ages. Her work has appeared in a variety of magazines, including *Boys Quest* and *Christian Home and School*. She and her husband live in Colorado Springs, Colorado, with their three children.